CONTEMPORARY AMERICAN SUCCESS STORIES

Famous People of Asian Ancestry
Volume II

Barbara J. Marvis

A Mitchell Lane
Multicultural Biography Series

CONTEMPORARY AMERICAN SUCCESS STORIES
Famous People of Asian Ancestry

VOLUME I
Pat Suzuki
Minoru Yamasaki
Kristi Yamaguchi
An Wang
Connie Chung
Carlos Bulosan

VOLUME II
Dalip Singh Saund
Patsy Takemoto Mink
Daniel Ken Inouye
Yoshiko Uchida
Haing Ngor

VOLUME III
Samuel I. Hayakawa
Vivian Kim
Isamu Noguchi
Ida Chen
Michael Chang

Design and Composition: SJS Associates

Library of Congress Catalog Card Number: 93-78991

P.O. Box 200
Childs, Maryland 21916

ISBN 1-883845-01-7 hardcover
ISBN 1-883845-07-6 softcover

TABLE OF CONTENTS

Acknowledgements

We wish to acknowledge with gratitude the generous co-operation of Congresswoman Patsy Mink for helping with the story of her life and graciously supplying us with photographs; Senator Daniel Inouye for taking the time to help us with his biography and for providing photographs; and Mary Jane Perna, co-executor for the estate of Yoshiko Uchida for allowing us permission to reprint her photographs.

Every reasonable effort has been made to seek copyright permission, where such permission has been deemed necessary. Any oversight brought to the publisher's attention will be corrected in future printings. Quotations reprinted from *Journey to Washington* by Senator Daniel Inouye with Lawrence Elliot, © 1967 reprinted by permission of the publisher, Prentice Hall/ a Division of Simon & Schuster, Englewood Cliffs, N.J. Quotations from *A Cambodian Odyssey* by Haing Ngor and Roger Warner reprinted with the permission of Macmillan Publishing Company. Copyright © 1987 by Sandwell Investment, Ltd. and Roger Warner. Quotations reprinted from *Desert Exile: The Uprooting of a Japanese American Family* by Yoshiko Uchida, © 1982, reprinted by permission of the publisher, The University of Washington Press.

Photo Credits

Cover, Barbara Marvis; p.8, UPI/Bettman; p.18, p.21, AP/Wide World Photos; p.22, p.25, p.29, p.32, p.36, p.39, courtesy Patsy Mink; p.40, p.44, p.48, p.57, courtesy Daniel Inouye; p.58, courtesy University of Washington Press by permission of Mary Jane Perna; p.61, p.63, p.66, p.69, by permission of Mary Jane Perna; p.76, p.94, AP/Wide World Photos.

PREFACE

More people live in Asia than on any other continent. The continent of Asia is located east of Europe. Asia is so large that the northern border touches the Arctic circle. It is divided by an imaginary line that runs from the Ural Mountains, to the Caspian Sea, and then through the Black Sea.

The people of Asia are divided into two races: Asian and Indian. The Asians include most of the people of China, Japan, Korea, Taiwan, Vietnam, Laos, Cambodia, the Philippines, and most of the other people in southeast Asia. The other major race is Indian. Most of the Indians came from India and the surrounding areas.

People all over the world have the same needs, but they meet these needs in different ways. They learned their way of thinking and acting from their ancestors. These traditions are called culture. People living in Asia have a distinct culture as do people living in many other parts of the world. People who came to America from Asia or other places may carry some of this culture to their new homeland. Then they learn new ways of doing things from other people in America. Some of their original traditions may change. Pretty soon, these immigrants are no longer Asians, but they are Americans. We sometimes refer to people by their ancestry, since most people are proud of their heritage. So this book refers to Asian Americans as people whose ancestors came from Asia. But, they are really all Americans, because everyone in the United States, except the Native Americans, has ancestors who originally came from somewhere else in the world. Even a first generation immigrant who makes his life in the United States, is an American.

Sometimes it is difficult to look at a person and tell where his or her ancestors might have come from. But certain people have distinctive looks that allow us to easily distinguish them from others. One of the problems that Americans of Asian ancestry have faced is that they are easily distinguished by their looks. The Asian Americans are often subjected to racism and ethnic prejudice as are other distinguishable groups of Americans. The Asians who came to America had many different customs and beliefs compared to people of other immigration groups. Not many Americans understood their way of life. So they have been met with prejudice and distrust over the years.

For many years, much of the Asian population were not permitted to come to the United States, or they were permitted in restricted numbers. The Chinese Exclusion Act of 1882 was among the first laws to effectively keep the Chinese and Japanese from emigrating to the U.S. The Immigration Act of 1924 prohibited any people who were not eligible for citizenship from coming to the United States. At that time, only Caucasians and black people of African descent were eligible for citizenship. The reason for the Exclusion Act was to preserve jobs for American workers that had been going to Asian immigrants.

During World War II, the Japanese Americans faced additional problems after Japan bombed Pearl Harbor, Hawaii. Some people said that the Japanese Americans in Hawaii helped Japan with the bombing. But, this is not so. The Japanese Americans contributed greatly to the war effort for America. Nevertheless, on February 19, 1942 President Franklin D. Roosevelt signed executive order number 9066, which relocated more than 110,000 Japanese Americans from the three westernmost states from their homes to centralized camps, most not fit for human inhabitation. Two-thirds of these people were American citizens born here in the United States. Most of the people in the camps were there only because they were unable to find other places to go before the mass-evacuation order was issued. There were ten relocation areas, managed by the civilian War Relocation Authority, in undeveloped regions of Arizona, California, Utah, Wyoming, Colorado, and Arkansas. Merely because of their race, these Japanese Americans were denied their rights as American citizens. Though the safety of the country was the reason for this relocation, it is not understood why German Americans were not also relocated during this time, since Germany was the main aggressor in World War II.

It was not until 1943 that President Roosevelt allowed young nisei (nee-sayee; second-generation Japanese American) young men to volunteer for service in the United States Army. Immediately, ten thousand Japanese American men, eighty-percent of those who were eligible, volunteered to prove their loyalty to *their* land. Many of these young men served in the famed, and much decorated 442nd Regimental Combat Team.

The people of the United States are descendants of a long migration. The roots of our nation reach out to all continents of the globe. We are a people woven of many strands. The mix of culture affects every aspect of our lives. Someday, we may all learn to live with one another, respecting our differences while treasuring the things we share.

This book chronicles the lives of five great Asian Americans who have made notable contributions to American society.

Black
Sea

Turkey

Syria

Iraq

Saudi
Arabia

Iran

Afghan-
istan

Pakistan

Commonwealth of Independent States

Ural
Mountains

Caspian Sea

Mongolia

China

North
Korea

South
Korea

Japan

PACIFIC OCEAN

Taiwan

(Myanmar)

Burma

Laos

India

ARABIAN
SEA

BAY
OF
BENGAL

Thai-
land

Cambodia

Vietnam

Philippines

Malaysia

Indonesia

ASIA

DALIP SINGH SAUND

Congressman from California, businessman
1899-1973

"His devotion to American principles is so strong, he has noted that even though he grew up in the ferment of India's independence movement, his early heroes were Washington and Lincoln and his inclination was to follow in their footsteps geographically, rather than Mahatma Gandhi. **"**

The New York Times, Saturday, November 10, 1956

AS YOU READ

- Dalip Saund came to the United States in 1920, but he was not eligible to run for Congress until nearly three decades later. Read to find out what prevented him from seeking a House seat?

- Dalip came from a well-to-do family in India, and could have been well-off if he stayed in India. Can you find out why he chose to come to the United States?

- Saund ran in the 1956 election against a very high profile female. See if you can find out what factors contributed to his success.

- When Saund was sent back to India on a good-will tour for the United States, how did the people of Asia treat him, considering he gave up his native homeland to live in America?

In the
spring of
1956,
Saund
announced
that he
was
thinking
of
running
for
Congress.
His
friends
told him
this might
not be a
good
idea.

DALIP SINGH SAUND

The Congressional battle for California's twenty-ninth district seat in the U.S. House of Representatives, was especially fierce in 1956. Dalip Singh Saund, a native of India who became a naturalized citizen of the United States in 1949, was running on the Democratic ticket against Republican contender Jacqueline Cochran Odlum, a world famous aviatrix, wife of a millionaire, and a friend of presidents and royalty. Though there were very few women in Congress at the time, there certainly were no Congresspersons of Indian, or of Asian descent, for that matter. And what was even more interesting, was the twenty-ninth district had always sent a Republican to Congress. The odds looked particularly bad for Saund, a farmer and owner of his own chemical fertilizer business in the Imperial Valley.

In the spring of 1956, Saund announced that he was thinking of running for Congress. His friends told him this might not be a good idea. They warned him that there might be prejudice because his skin was too dark. Of the thirty-four newspapers in the area, only four small weeklies supported him. The district was made up of Imperial and Riverside counties, with a population at that time of 285,000. Geographically, it was one of the country's largest districts—about the size of Massachusetts, Rhode Island, and Delaware combined. Saund and his family traveled every road of the two counties (over

DALIP SINGH SAUND

11,000 square miles) to campaign for his election. He spent $20,000 on his campaign and carried both counties by a majority of four-thousand votes to be elected to the eighty-fifth Congress. People said, "We believe what Dalip Saund said, and *he* believed what he said."

"I met resistance," Saund said when he was campaigning, "but only as a Democrat. Discrimination? Absolutely none."

Dalip Singh Saund was born on September 20, 1899, in the village of Chhajalwadi in northern India. Chhajalwadi is near the Punjab city of Amritsar. His grandfather was a village blacksmith, with no assets but five husky boys. The boys left home to make a better life for themselves. His father and two brothers became well off. His parents, Natha Singh Saund and Jeoni (Kaur) Saund, were Sikhs–an Indian sect that separated from the Hindus more than five hundred years ago. This religious group was known for their prowess as warriors and for their beliefs that opposed the caste system, where some people were better than others. His parents were well-to-do landowners and government contractors for canals and railroads. Though neither of his parents could read or write, they valued education for their children.

Saund said, "It is a western delusion that women occupy an inferior position in India; ac-

> "It is a western delusion that women occupy an inferior position in India; actually, my mother was always the boss of the family..."

tually, my mother was always the boss of the family. My father died when I was ten."

Saund attended grammar school and high school in Amritsar and was graduated with honors from the University of Punjab in 1919. The obvious next step for an intelligent, well-educated Sikh would have been to take a position in Britain's Indian civil service. (India was under British rule at that time.) But Dalip was America-inclined. He had heard of Woodrow Wilson, who wanted to make the world safe for democracy, and from Wilson's speeches, he learned of the writings of Abraham Lincoln. So, about the time that Gandhi and Nehru went to prison in India, Dalip headed for the United States to attend the University of California. He decided he would study the canning industry in the United States and would then return to India to set up a profitable business.

In 1920, Dalip Singh Saund enrolled in the University of California at Berkeley. He lived with about eighty other Indian students and enrolled for several agricultural classes. He found out that if he took a few math classes, he could get his master's degree. Eventually, he went on to get his doctorate in mathematics. While he studied food preservation, he also worked each summer in California canning factories. He received his M.A. degree in Mathematics in 1922, and his Ph.d. in 1924. "Here I was a free man in a free country. I could go where I wished

> "Here I was a free man in a free country. I could go where I wished and say what I pleased."

and say what I pleased," said Saund, who was very happy to spend this time in America.

An elder brother had been supporting Dalip while he was in the United States. But after he died, there were no more checks coming from home, and Dalip was on his own. Saund had frequently spoken before student and church groups while at Berkeley. He was very critical of British rule in India. His family heard of his anti-British tirades. Saund was not sure what he should do about his future. He did not know if he wanted to return to India. "At that time, in 1924, India was in revolt. Gandhi and Nehru were in and out of jail. I thought, why go back—to jail."

"I was riding off in all directions. I wanted to write a history of India, be a teacher, return to India as a political fighter, make a fortune. I was adrift in a country where I could not become a citizen, and my first job after earning a Ph.d. was as foreman of the syrup department in a fruit cannery. I never used my math again."

Saund had attended religious services at the Sikh temple at Stockton, in the San Joaquin Valley. There he met many Hindus who drove big cars. They were all farmers in the rich, irrigated Imperial Valley. So the second job that this Ph.d. from Berkeley got was that of a foreman of a cotton-picking gang near Holtville. He earned very good money, saved it, and planted a good celery crop by sharecropping—and then lost everything he owned. This was merely the first bet Saund made in the unpredictable agricultural market.

> He earned good money, saved it, and planted a good celery crop by share-cropping—and then lost everything he owned.

Before Saund settled down to full-time farming, however, he wanted to write a book. Katherine Mayo had just published a best-seller, *Mother India,* in 1927, which was an ill-reported picture of India's backwardness. Saund went to Los Angeles to research his book, *My Mother India,* which was published in 1930 by Hertzel. The book was not a financial success.

While Saund was in Los Angeles working on his book, he met Emil Kosa, Jr., a young artist who heard Saund speak at the First Unitarian Society of Hollywood. Emil invited Dalip to dinner at his home on Sunset Boulevard and introduced him to his pretty, blonde, nineteen-year-old sister, Marian. Marian, who was born in Cape Cod, Massachusetts, was then a freshman at the University of California at Los Angeles (UCLA). They liked each other right away. They were married in 1928, only six months after they first met! Marian helped Dalip with his book. Though the book had disappointing sales, 1930 was a good year for the Saunds, for their first son, Dalip, Jr. was born then. They eventually had two more children, Julie, and Ellie.

So the Saunds returned to the Imperial Valley to resume farming. The future Congressman did most of his farming around Westmorland. He tried to grow everything–alfalfa, lettuce, melons, onions, celery, cotton, sugar beets, and Punjab flax. Dalip was not permitted to become a citizen at that time, and thus, was not allowed to own or lease land. He was able to lease land in his wife's name, however, since she was an American citizen born in the United States. Sometimes he could sharecrop with someone else who wasn't allowed to own land, either.

Though the market was always unpredictable, the Saunds generally made enough money to buy a new car every year, and to take their children on vacations. In the 1930's, the Imperial Valley had many bad seasons. One year, crickets destroyed their crops. The next it was mildew. Then the blackbirds came. In the mid-1930's, Saund did very well one year with alfalfa. He took all his profits, and borrowed additional money from the bank to increase his holdings. The next season, the bottom fell out of the market and the Saund's went broke. Dalip was advised to declare bankruptcy like all the other farmers were doing. "In India," Saund said, "a man who takes bankruptcy must keep a coal-oil lamp burning in his window as a symbol of his shame." Bankruptcy was a big disgrace to Saund; some people who Dalip owed money to got judgments against him. Still, he did not file for bankruptcy; it took him many years, but he paid off all his debts.

> ...It took him many years, but he paid off all his debts.

DALIP SINGH SAUND

In 1942, the family doctor told Marian Saund that she could no longer live in the Imperial Valley. She had bad asthma that was aggravated by various grasses and weeds in the area. Dalip and his son built the family a three-bedroom home, and Marian and the children moved to Los Angeles. Dalip traveled back and forth. Marian Saund returned to school, graduated in 1945, and became a teacher. It was difficult for Dalip to be so far from his family. Mostly, he could only see them on weekends. But he occupied his time helping to organize the India Association of America, which pushed for legislation that would make his three thousand fellow countrymen eligible for citizenship. Saund went to Washington, D.C. to urge the adoption of an amendment to the immigration law. Clare Boothe Luce, a Republican, and Emanuel Cellar, a Democrat, sponsored the bill. President Truman signed the bill into law in 1946, and Saund immediately applied for citizenship. It took three years until he got his naturalization papers.

When Saund became a citizen, he was immediately appointed to the central committee of the Democratic Party in the Imperial Valley, and became chairman. He also decided to run for town judge in Westmorland, which is like a justice of the peace. Saund passed an examination that was required by the state, even though he was not a lawyer. He won the election in 1950; but, five Westmorland citizens petitioned to have him disqualified because he had not been a citizen for a full year. Saund did not to oppose the petition.

The County Board of Supervisors then had to appoint a new judge. Hundreds of Westmorland citizens asked that Dalip be appointed since by that time, he had been a citizen for a year. But the Board appointed Frank Lyall, whom Saund easily defeated in the next election. In 1953, he assumed the office of judge of the justice court. He was a very dedicated judge, and he gave much of his attention to cleaning up prostitution, drugs, and gambling in Westmorland. About this same time, he set up his chemical fertilizer business.

In 1956, Saund set about to win a seat in the United States House of Representatives. His family campaigned for him regularly throughout the two counties. Saund argued that his victory would show the world that prejudice does not prevail in the United States. He also wanted to help better relations between Asia and the United States. Saund got heavy support from the district's minority groups—Mexican Americans, African Americans, and a few East Indians. He also won the farm vote and did well in the cities. He received 54,989 votes to his competitor's 51,690.

Just a few days after Saund arrived in Washington for the eighty-fifth Congress, the Demo-

Saund argued that his victory would show the world that prejudice does not prevail in the United States.

DALIP SINGH SAUND

crats placed him on the House Foreign Affairs Committee. This was an honor for a first-term Congressman. He was assigned by the committee to survey the United States foreign aid program in Asia. This gave him a chance to return to India to deny the propaganda that the Communists were spreading about the United States.

Saund campaigned every road in Imperial and Riverside counties.

On October 22, 1957, Saund and his family began their good-will trip to Asia. (Marian took a sabbatical from teaching for a year.) "When we took off from San Francisco I was worried," Saund said. "I had not been back to India since I'd left thirty-seven years before. I had renounced by Indian birthright for

American citizenship. Would I be welcomed or booed?"

The Saunds were met with cheers everywhere they went. Dalip talked to the chiefs of state or ministers of a dozen nations. He sometimes made up to eight speeches in one day. He had to answer some difficult questions about the United States, and he answered them truthfully. Everywhere he went, he found that propaganda spread by the Soviet Union was rampant. Russia constantly told Europe and Asia that minority groups were oppressed in the United States. Saund told them that he was living proof that any person can accomplish what they want in the United States. "Here am I, a living example of American democracy. I was chosen by the people in a free election," he told his listeners. But Saund always felt that the United States did not do a very good job with its own public relations. "Before giving aid to a country," Saund said, "let us first spend some of that money to tell them our motives–that the American people are paying through the nose in high taxes to save the democratic way of life and the free world."

When Dalip returned to his native village, there were people lined up for miles to see him. His brother, Karnail, provided him with a private railroad car. In New Delhi, three days before his departure home, he was invited to address the joint session of the Houses of Parliament. He was given a standing ovation. Then Prime Min-

"Here am I, a living example of American democracy. I was chosen by the people in a free election."

ister Nehru, whom Saund had met the year before in Washington, hosted a private family luncheon for the Saunds. "The invitation to address Parliament and the receptions everywhere were a tribute not to D.S. Saund, but to the American people," Saund said. "The thrilling fact is that throughout Asia, and especially in India, the people hold America in such great esteem, they are proud that one of them has been freely elected to the United States Congress." The Saunds returned home on January 3 from their good-will tour.

Dalip Saund, a stocky man with dark eyes, thick, black hair, and dark skin was a controversial figure in Congress. There were those who liked him very much, and those who did not like him at all. He was a very patient man; his own son described him as the most patient man he knew. In his lifetime, his son had said, he'd never seen his father lose his temper.

Saund was re-elected to Congress in 1958 and again in 1960. While he was campaigning for the 1962 election, he suffered a massive stroke. Although he continued to campaign from his hospital bed, he lost his bid for re-election. A second stroke on April 23, 1973 was fatal.

DALIP SINGH SAUND

Dalip and Marian Saund

PATSY TAKEMOTO MINK

1927-
Congresswoman from Hawaii

❝I just live for the day when people will look at me and simply call me an American. I feel, act, and live like any other American the country over.**❞**

Patsy Mink

- Why do you think Patsy Mink would rather be called simply "an American," rather than a "Japanese American?" See if you can tell from the story.

- Many Asian Americans enter interracial marriages. Patsy Mink's husband, John, was not of Japanese descent. Read to find out how her parents felt about this.

- Can you find out what issues Patsy Mink has dedicated her time to in Congress?

- In 1976, Mink lost her bid for a Senate seat. Find out how she was able to return to Congress in 1990.

PATSY TAKEMOTO MINK

In 1964, Patsy Mink became the first woman from Hawaii to be elected to the United States House of Representatives. She is also the first woman of Japanese ancestry to serve there and the first woman of color in the entire Congress. She has long been the most prominent woman in Hawaiian politics and has been a champion of civil rights for women and minorities and of federal aid to education. Articulate and outspoken, Patsy Mink has taken firm stands on such controversial issues as the Vietnam war, nuclear testing, and excessive government secrecy. As a result, she has both loyal admirers and some angry critics!

Patsy Matsu Takemoto was born on December 6, 1927, in the village of Paia on the Hawaiian Island of Maui. Soon after, her family moved to Hamakuapoko, which had about three hundred homes at the time. The Takemotos lived in a comfortable house on two acres of land. The family had pigs, chickens, rabbits, and turkeys, and enjoyed a comfortable lifestyle that most other Japanese Americans on Hawaii did not share at that time.

Patsy was one of two children born to Suematsu Takemoto and Mitama (Tateyama) Takemoto. She has a brother, Eugene, who is a year older than she. She and Eugene had a very happy childhood, roaming the mountains to pick edible fruits and bamboo shoots. Patsy and Eu-

> Both of Patsy's parents were born in Hawaii and were nisei who spoke English at home. Patsy and Eugene are sansei, or third-generation Americans.

gene were close friends and Eugene would include Patsy in his football and baseball games. Later in life, Eugene helped Patsy with her election campaigns.

Both of Patsy's parents were born in Hawaii and were nisei, (nee-sayee, second-generation Japanese American) who spoke English at home. Patsy and Eugene are sansei, or third-generation Americans. Her father, Suematsu, was a land surveyor for the East Maui Irrigation Company. He earned a degree in civil engineering from the University of Hawaii, the first American of Japanese ancestry to achieve this distinction at the University of Hawaii. It was his good position as a civil engineer that provided the family with a comfortable lifestyle. However, Suematsu was subjected to the type of discrimination that is still common in many workplaces today. He was constantly passed over for a promotion to the "all-white" managerial staff, and was often humiliated when he was asked to train the new manager, who was usually white and younger than he. After

From left to right, Eugene, Mitama, and Patsy (taken in 1986)

this had happened several times, Suematsu surprised everyone by resigning his position and moving the family to Honolulu to set up his own land surveying company.

At age four, Patsy insisted that she was ready to start school, even though she was too young. With special permission from the principal, Patsy attended Hamakuapoko school in her own program. When she was in fourth grade, Patsy and Eugene transferred to Kaunoa English Standard School. Suematsu's superiors at work suggested that he enroll his children there. At that time, Hawaii had a dual system of public education: one for white children and another for "non-whites." A child could only go to an English Standard School if they passed an admissions test. The test was based on how well the student spoke English. This quite obviously left out a lot of first-generation immigrants. Patsy and Eugene passed the entrance exam easily, but they found the new school was unfriendly. They had to travel a great distance to get to school and none of their classmates lived nearby.

Patsy later attended Maui High School where she was president of the student body in her senior year. Patsy decided to run against one of her best friends, Harriette Holt. "Like most of the decisions I've made in politics, it seemed like a good idea at the time," said Patsy. "Why not? The football team backed me, that's why I won."

> At that time, Hawaii had a dual system of public education: one for white children and another for "non-whites."

PATSY TAKEMOTO MINK

When the Japanese attacked Pearl Harbor on December 7, 1941, Patsy was a sophomore at Maui High. The war affected all of their lives. Many of the Japanese Americans living in Hawaii were afraid that they would be associated with the enemy. The Japanese community was full of fear and shame for something they had no part in.

World War II was still going on when Patsy graduated as valedictorian of her class in 1944. She enrolled at the University of Hawaii in Honolulu as a pre-med student. From the time she was four, Patsy thought she would be a doctor. No one ever told her she couldn't, even though the field was dominated by white males. At the end of her second year at the University of Hawaii, Patsy discovered that many of her friends were transferring to colleges on the mainland, and she did not want to be left behind. She applied to a small women's college, Wilson College, in Chambersburg, Pennsylvania.

When she arrived in the fall of her junior year, she had to meet with the president. He explained to her that since English was not her first language, she would probably have a hard time with her studies. He went on to tell her that he would make an exception for her and give her a private room so that she would not have to share with anyone. Patsy was astonished by this. However, when the president realized that En-

The
International
House was
not only for
foreign
students
from India,
Turkey, etc.,
but also for
Americans
who were
Black, Asian,
and
Hispanic.

glish was indeed her first language, he changed his mind. He said, "Oh, you speak English...well, in that case, you'll share a room with another student." But the atmosphere at Wilson College was not to Patsy's liking, and after one semester, she made plans to transfer to the University of Nebraska.

Patsy found that the University of Nebraska was no better than Wilson College. The college subjected her to much racism. At first, Patsy was pleased to find that she would be living in the International House on campus. But she quickly became angry when she learned that the university had a housing policy that separated whites from students of color. The International House was not only for foreign students from India, Turkey, etc., but also for Americans who were Black, Asian, and Hispanic. Only white students could live in the school dormitories and in the sorority and fraternity houses. Patsy engaged in a personal crusade to change this discriminatory policy, and that very year, the board of regents rescinded the previous segregationist policy.

While at the University of Nebraska, Patsy developed a serious thyroid condition and she had to have an operation. She decided to go back to Hawaii and finish her studies there. She completed her final year at the University of Hawaii, and graduated in 1948 with a B.A. degree in zoology and chemistry. In the spring of

1948, Patsy applied to more than twelve medical schools. At that time, there were very few women in medicine. To make matters worse, many men were returning from the war and the schools had too many applications. So Patsy could not get into medical school. Though she was disappointed, she did not let this stop her. In July 1948, she applied to the University of Chicago law school, and set her sights on a new career. The University of Chicago accepted her under its "foreign student quota," even though she was an American citizen, born in the Territory of Hawaii. Again, Patsy did not let this deter her, but quickly left for Chicago.

Patsy and John Mink in 1988

At the University of Chicago, Patsy met her husband, John Francis Mink. He was from Pennsylvania and was doing graduate work in geophysics. They married on January 27, 1951, just six months after they met. Patsy's parents had wanted her to wait until she got her law degree before she considered marriage. Her parents also did not approve of John's racial background. The interracial marriage was not well accepted

On January 4, 1965, she was sworn in by Speaker John McCormack as the first Asian American female and the first woman of color elected to the House of Representatives.

at that time. Once again, this did not deter Patsy, who automatically followed her own instincts.

After Patsy received her doctor of law degree and John received his M.A. in geophysics, the Minks went looking for jobs. John found a job quickly with United States Steel Corporation. But, for Patsy, being a female, Asian American lawyer made it impossible for her to find employment. In 1952, their daughter, Gwendolyn Rachel (Wendy) was born, and the Minks decided to go back to Patsy's homeland in Hawaii. John Mink found a position with the Hawaii Sugar Planters Association, and Mrs. Mink opened her own, private law practice. She also lectured on business law at the University of Hawaii and served as attorney of the Hawaii House of Representatives in 1955.

Patsy became involved in politics in 1954 when she founded and became the first president of the Oahu Young Democrats. Two years later, she was elected the first territorial president of the Hawaii Young Democrats. In 1956, she decided to run for a seat in the territorial House of Representatives. "I faced overwhelming odds," said Patsy, "I was not from a political family, and I had no visible support in the community, no organizational support." Many people did not believe she could be elected. But, that did not stop her. She went out campaigning, door-to-door and was elected to the

PATSY TAKEMOTO MINK

Hawaii House of Representatives by a wide margin. In 1958 and again in 1962, she was elected to the Hawaii Senate. In 1960, she was a delegate to the Democratic National Convention where she was a member of the platform committee that helped to negotiate a civil rights plank in the Democratic platform that year.

After Hawaii was made a state, Patsy Mink tried to gain the Democratic nomination for the at-large seat in the House of Representatives. She lost to Daniel Inouye, whom you will read about later in this book. She tried again in 1964 and won. (After the 1960 census, Hawaii became eligible for a second seat in the House. Hawaii still has only two seats today.) Daniel Inouye was elected to the Senate in 1962 and Spark Matsunaga was already in office with one House seat. "Getting elected took a lot of island-hopping," Mink said, "and sometimes five coffee hours in one evening–but it was festive, too." Throughout her campaign, Patsy treasured a special papier mache doll whose eyes, by tradition, are not painted on until its owner gets their secret wish. "I painted one eye in after the primary, the other when I was elected to Congress." On January 4, 1965, she was sworn in by Speaker John McCormack as the first Asian American female and the first woman of color elected to the House of Representatives.

During her years in Congress, she concentrated on the same issues that had been the focus of her attention in the state legislature. Among the many educational acts she introduced or sponsored were the first child care bill and legislation establishing bilingual education. She was also responsible for legislation expanding the federal student loan program, special education, and headstart programs.

From left to right, Patsy's parents, Suematsu and Mitama Takemoto, her daughter Gwendolyn, and Patsy and husband John taken after the 1964 election.

When Lyndon Johnson was President, Mink was a strong supporter of his domestic program, but she was a very early critic of the military buildup in Vietnam. In 1967, she refused to support the President in his request for a tax increase because she felt that the additional monies would be used for military action in Vietnam. In her newsletter to her district she wrote, "$78 billion, or one-half of our federal tax revenues, are now expended in support of our military efforts. $30 billion of this is devoted to our Vietnam effort—over $1500 for each man, woman, and child in

PATSY TAKEMOTO MINK

South Vietnam! By coincidence this is approximately the amount of the deficit in the federal budget–$28 billion–which now prompts the administration to urge a tax increase. However, the tax increase is projected to raise only $6 billion this year, or less than a fourth of the amount needed. Thus the tax increase will in no way give assurance that the funds so sorely needed for domestic programs in education, poverty, social welfare, and urban development will be available."

When President Nixon nominated G. Harrold Carswell to the Supreme Court, Mink was a very early critic, pointing out that he had denied women's employment rights when he was an appellate judge. In 1970, she testified before the Senate Judiciary Committee against him. Carswell was not confirmed.

One of Mink's most far-reaching accomplishments in Congress came while Nixon was President, when she challenged government secrecy. In 1971, the Atomic Energy Commission authorization bill included plans for a secret project to detonate an underground nuclear explosion at Amchitka Island in the Aleutian Islands. Patsy was afraid that the explosion might do damage to Hawaii, and she tried to defeat the funding for the project and remove authority for the tests.

With the test date quickly approaching, Patsy asked to see copies of important government

One of Mink's most far-reaching accomplishments in Congress came while Nixon was President, when she challenged government secrecy.

reports about the secret project. Her request was denied. The president's counsel said the reports were "sensitive" and "vital...to national defense." On August 11, 1971, Patsy filed suit with twenty-three other Congressmen to make the government disclose the reports under the Freedom of Information Act in *Mink v. Environmental Protection Agency, et al.* The issue of the case was whether the president could withhold information as "secret" without review by the courts or the legislature to determine if the documents indeed needed to be kept secret.

Ramsey Clark, former U.S. attorney and a law school classmate, agreed to serve as counsel on the case, without charge. The U.S. District Court determined that the documents did not have to be disclosed because they were exempt from the Freedom of Information Act. Mink appealed. The U.S. Court of Appeals reversed the decision and sent it back to District Court to determine if some of the documents should be revealed. They also suggested that Congress pass a new law requiring review of "sensitive" material in order to allow its release.

In 1974, the Congress amended the Freedom of Information Act to allow release of certain sensitive documents. President Gerald Ford vetoed the bill, but Congress overrode his veto. This case gained tremendous historical significance when it was cited by the U.S. Supreme

Court as a precedent for releasing the Watergate tapes.

Patsy Mink was successfully returned to Congress in each election (six terms), until, in 1976, she decided to seek the Democratic nomination for the U.S. Senate rather than run for a seventh term in the House. U.S. Senator Hiram L. Fong had announced his intention to retire. She lost the election to Spark Matsunaga.

From 1976 to 1989, Patsy Mink remained active in government and politics. In 1977, President Jimmy Carter nominated Patsy as Assistant Secretary of State for Oceans and International Environmental and Scientific Affairs. She served in this capacity in 1977 and 1978. For the next three years, she served as president of the Americans for Democratic Action. When she returned to Hawaii in 1980, she found that it had changed. She found many problems of crime, energy, and sewage disposal. She decided to return to politics, and in 1982, she was elected to the Honolulu City Council where she served from 1983 to 1987.

In 1990, Patsy Mink returned to the U.S. House of Representatives when she won a special election held on September 22. In 1990, Spark Matsunaga died, and Governor Waihee appointed Daniel Akaka to replace Matsunaga in the Senate. Akaka had represented the second district, but he resigned when he was appointed to the Senate, leaving the House position vacant.

Gwendolyn, Patsy, and John Mink celebrate on election night, September 22, 1990

Campaigning on the slogan, "The Experience of a Lifetime," Patsy met a lot of opposition. Some people thought she was too old to go back to Congress. She won, nevertheless, and was elected six weeks later to a full term. She was re-elected again in 1992. She again serves on the Committee on Education and Labor and is also a member of the Committee on Government Operations. In addition, she was elected by the members of the House to serve on the U.S. House Budget Committee beginning in 1993.

In the one-hundred second and one-hundred third Congresses (1990-1991; 1992-1993), Mink currently serves on three education subcommittees: postsecondary education; elementary, secondary, and vocational education; and Labor-Management Relations. She is attempting to put a college education within financial reach of more people and is dedicated to helping America's youth become the world's best in science and math. In October 1991, she introduced the "Incentives for Educational Excellence Act," a comprehensive education reform bill to improve education from preschool through high school. The bill authorizes full funding of headstart programs and would increase current federal funding levels of elementary and secondary education by $5 billion each year for the next five years.

The issues of jobs and unemployment are also of importance to her. She was the first member of Congress to introduce legislation (H.R. 1518) to reform the emergency unemployment system to provide an automatic twenty-six weeks of benefits to those out of work in states with unemployment rates higher than six per-

Patsy Takemoto Mink

cent. Legislation similar to that she introduced was adopted by the House on June 6, 1992 and signed into law on July 3, 1992.

Petite at five feet and one-inch with brown eyes and black hair, Patsy Mink and her husband, John, live in Washington and continue to maintain their home in Hawaii. Their daughter, Wendy, is grown and is an associate professor of political science at the University of California at Santa Cruz.

Patsy Mink has won numerous awards in her long political career. The Outstanding Woman in Politics award was given to her in 1965 by the District of Columbia Business and Professional Women's Association. She has also been honored by the Japanese American Citizens League, the Overseas Education Association, the National Education Association, and the National Multiple Sclerosis Society. On August 9, 1992, she was awarded the 1992 Margaret Brent Women Lawyers of Achievement Award by the American Bar Association's Commission on Women in the Profession.

It is quite evident that Patsy Mink has worked hard to improve the lives of all Americans. Her work in government will have lasting effects well into the twenty-first century.

PATSY TAKEMOTO MINK

The Mink family portrait

DANIEL KEN INOUYE

Democratic Senior Senator from Hawaii
1924-

66**I**t was in my sophomore year...that I first came under the warm and rewarding spell of Mrs. Ruth King...

66 All at once literature was exciting and history was real. Washington and Jefferson and Lincoln suddenly stepped out of some mythical haze...I felt the bitter cold and despair of that winter at Valley Forge. I felt a sharp sense of personal loss at the death of Lincoln... Whereas Japanese history had always sounded like some impersonal pageant, the story of America had the ring of an adventure in human progress...

66 But most important of all, I came to believe that the giants who made American history were *my* forefathers. Always before, I had been a little embarrassed singing about the 'land where my fathers died...' It was Mrs. King who, in some wonderfully subtle way convinced me of the essential relationship between America's founding fathers and all of America's people. 99

Excerpt from *Journey to Washington,* (Prentice-Hall), Daniel K. Inouye

AS YOU READ

- As you read, keep in mind that Daniel Inouye was born as an American citizen. But all through his life, he has had to prove his loyalty to this country. Look for some of the ways he has proven his loyalty.

- Inouye attended a Japanese-language school in addition to the neighborhood public schools. He later dropped out of the Japanese-language school. Read to find out why.

DANIEL KEN INOUYE

Daniel Ken Inouye, the Democratic Senior Senator from Hawaii, the first American of Japanese descent to be elected to the United States Senate, dropped out of college in 1943 to volunteer for the newly formed 442nd Regimental Combat Team. He was among the first of more than ten thousand nisei (second-generation Japanese American) young men who volunteered to enlist in the United States Army. This unit was the first all-nisei combat group authorized by Congress because the young Japanese Americans insisted they be allowed to prove their loyalty to the United States. The now-famous combat team, who declared "Go For Broke" as their battle cry, fought their way through Italy and France.

Two days before the war in Europe ended, the 442nd regiment was charging up the hills around the Po Valley in Italy. After circling and destroying an enemy observation post, Inouye's platoon was about 40 yards from the main German defenses. They moved in closer. All at once, three enemy machine guns caught the platoon out in the open and began a merciless crossfire. Inouye pulled the pin on a grenade and started running toward the nearest machine gun bunker. An enemy bullet pierced through his stomach and came out his back, barely missing his spine. Hardly noticing the pain, he kept inching toward the machine gun nest, which had had his men pinned down. He somehow managed to throw two grenades before his right arm was shattered by a German rifle grenade at close range. He then tossed a third grenade with his left hand into another enemy machine gun nest, saving his entire unit from almost certain death.

For his bravery, on that and other occasions, he was awarded the Distinguished Service Cross (the nation's second-highest military decoration), the Bronze Star, and the Purple Heart with two oak leaf clusters, and other honors. Few memorials have been dedicated to the Army's 442nd Regimental Combat Team. Only a handful of books on World War II even mention the unit in detail. But the men in this team suffered three hundred percent casualties and earned more decorations for battlefield bravery than any other unit its size. Lieutenant Inouye spent the next two years recovering in Army hospitals. His right arm had to be amputated. He retired from the Army as a Captain in 1947. On July 26, 1948, President Truman outlawed all discrimination in the Armed Forces, ending the practice of creating all-ethnic units. From then on, all American forces would be ALL-American.

Born in Honolulu, Hawaii on September 7, 1924, Daniel Ken Inouye is the oldest of four children born to Hyotaro and Kame (Imanaga) Inouye. He has a younger sister, Mae Masako, and two younger brothers, John and Robert. In his book, *Journey To Washington,* Inouye tells

Few memorials have been dedicated to the Army's 442nd Regimental Combat Team. Only a handful of books on World War II even mention the unit in detail.

DANIEL KEN INOUYE

The Inouye children, from left to
right, Dan, Mae, John, and Robert

how his ancestors struggled to reclaim their honor by settling a long-owed debt. A fire had started in the home of his great-grandfather in southern Japan. This fire also destroyed two other homes. Tradition required that his great-grandfather pay the cost of the damage (about $400), so he sent his son, Asakichi, Daniel's grandfather, to Hawaii in 1899, to live and earn the money to pay the debt.

Asakichi worked in sugar fields for about $12.50 a month. Asakichi and his wife had a son, Hyotaro, who was Daniel's father. Thirty years later, which was when Daniel was about five years old, Asakichi sent the last dollars home to repay the debt. This allowed his ancestors to again be respected in Japan. But, when Asakichi went to visit his family some years after the debt was repaid, he found that he was treated as though he had come back from the dead. Asakichi decided to remain in Hawaii, since he felt this was his true homeland.

Inouye describes his childhood as having been spent "in respectable poverty." Years later, the street on which he was born became the site of Honolulu's first slum clearance project. He didn't wear shoes regularly until he was in high school, and as far as he remembered when he was a child, all the other mothers in the neighborhood sliced a single hard-boiled egg to feed a family of six for breakfast.

> Inouye describes his childhood as having been spent "in respectable poverty."

Daniel Ken Inouye

Inouye attended both public school and a special Japanese-language school. The neighborhood that he grew up in was largely composed of Asian Americans, and much of his English was mixed with Japanese, Chinese, Hawaiian, and some exotic combinations of each. Most of his friends dropped out of the Japanese-language school after tenth grade, but Inouye agreed to enroll again in eleventh grade. The year was 1939 and things had already gotten very tense in Europe and the Far East.

"The Japanese government was in the iron grip of fanatic warlords and the Imperial Army was waging aggressive war in China and menacing all of Southeast Asia," recalls Dan. "Day after day, the priest who taught us ethics and Japanese history hammered away at the divine prerogatives of the Emperor, and at the grand destiny that called on the Japanese people to extend their sway over the yellow race, and on the madness that was inducing the American government to oppose them. He would tilt his menacing crew-cut skull at us and solemnly proclaim, 'You must remember that only a trick of fate has brought you so far from your homeland, but there must be no question of your loyalty. When Japan calls, you must know that it is Japanese blood that flows in your veins.'"

Inouye had heard these speeches many times. One day, his teacher had been discussing how inadequate Christianity was compared to

Shintoism, the state religion of Japan. Inouye shouted, "That's not right! That's not fair! I am a Christian, a lot of us here are, and you mustn't talk that way! I respect your faith. You must respect mine."

"How dare you!" his teacher roared.

"I do. I do dare you! You have no right to make fun of my beliefs."

"You are a Japanese! You will believe what I..."

"I am an American!"

> "I am an American!"

With that, his teacher picked him up bodily and threw him into the schoolyard. When he returned home, his mother expected an explanation. After she bandaged his knees, she took him back to the Japanese school. She went directly to the office of the principal. "I do not send him here to become a Shintoist or a samurai. I want him to learn the language and traditions of his ancestors, but we are Americans and shall always remain so," she told the principal. Inouye chose not to return to the Japanese-language school.

In December of 1941, when Japan bombed Pearl Harbor, it changed Inouye's life forever. Like so many other Japanese Americans, Inouye froze in horror when he saw the Japanese

DANIEL KEN INOUYE

planes; he was certain they must be German planes! But, they were not. By that time, the Japanese made up nearly forty percent of Hawaii's population. Hawaii was an American territorial possession at that time, but the people

Dan (center) with parents Hyotaro and Kame Inouye

living there were American citizens. "It was painful," recalled Inouye, "because I knew the people flying those planes looked just like me."

Though most of the Japanese living in Hawaii were not affected by the relocation of the Japanese Americans on the mainland just weeks after the bombing of Pearl Harbor, some fifteen hundred Japanese were rounded up on Hawaii and put in special camps. From the very beginning, the younger Japanese on the Islands felt a deep sense of personal disgrace. They could never quite convince the American government that the bombing of Pearl Harbor was not meant for only sixty percent of the population. The War Department turned down all Japanese Americans for active duty. However, the Japanese Americans found many other ways to serve their country.

Inouye graduated from McKinley High School in 1942, in the middle of World War II, and enrolled in the pre-medical program at the University of Hawaii. He decided he wanted to be a doctor. In 1943, the War Department finally announced that it would accept four thousand nisei volunteers to form a full-fledged combat unit, without restrictions, and without constraints. The outfit was to be activated on February 1.

"It is hard to express our emotions," writes Inouye, "at this expression of faith by the President. It was as though someone had let us out

In 1943, the War Department finally announced it would accept four thousand nisei volunteers to form a full-fledged combat unit...

> "It is hard to express our emotions," writes Inouye, "at this expression of faith by the President. It was as though someone had let us out of some dark place and into the sunlight again."

of some dark place and into the sunlight again." So Inouye temporarily dropped out of college and enlisted in the United States Army. When he was discharged in 1947 with the rank of captain, he re-enrolled at the University of Hawaii on the GI bill. Though he had intended to study medicine, the loss of his right arm caused him to reconsider this choice, and he chose to study law instead.

Inouye met his wife, Margaret Awamura, while he was at college, and decided he would marry her before they were even formally introduced! She was a teacher at the University. "I met her November 15, 1947," Dan remembers. "Our first date was November 22, a Thanksgiving dinner-dance at the Fort Shafter Officer's Club." On his second date on December 6, he proposed to Maggie in the car. On June 12, 1949, Dan and Margaret were married with nearly four hundred and fifty guests in attendance!

Inouye earned a B.A. degree in 1950 from the University of Hawaii and went on to study law at the George Washington University Law School in Washington, D.C. Maggie soon found a job with the Navy Bureau of Yards and Docks. Inouye's interests turned to politics as he served as a volunteer for the Democratic National Committee while at George Washington University. Of his years at George Washington University, Inouye says the school accorded him all of the courtesies and they were very good to him. Throughout the years, he has remained a friend of The George Washington University, serving on the University's Board of Trustees from 1981 to 1991. But Inouye remembers that the day after he arrived on campus, he wanted to get out.

"George Washington, unbeknownst to me, was segregated. Of course, the University desegregated in the early 1950's and has a good ethnic mix nowadays," he told Robert Guldin in a recent interview for *The George Washington University Magazine*. "But I recall the day after going through the registration ritual, visiting the assistant dean of the law school–I just happened to casually mention, 'I don't see any Blacks here–why is that?' He hemmed and hawed a little and he finally came out and said that we don't admit Black students. He pointed out that GW did accept students from Ethiopia because for some reason they were considered Aryan. Now you explain that to me! So, I seriously thought about leaving but then it was too late to go to any other school, the rolls were closed. So I decided to stay and make the best of it."

Inouye returned to Honolulu in 1952, after he received his law degree. He was appointed an assistant public prosecutor of Honolulu in 1953. The following year, he was elected to the territorial house of representatives in Hawaii, where he became the majority leader. In 1958, he became a member of the territorial senate.

DANIEL KEN INOUYE

In 1959, Hawaii became the fiftieth state and Inouye thought of running for the United States Senate. He actually entered the race, but then withdrew. He opted for a better chance to go to Washington. That same year, he won election to Hawaii's first seat in the House of Representatives (eighty-sixth Congress), with the largest number of votes ever cast for a candidate in Hawaii until then. He became the first Japanese American ever to serve in Congress. He was re-elected to the eighty-seventh Congress and served in the House of Representatives until he was elected to the Senate in 1962. In the Senate, he held the third-ranking Democratic leadership post–secretary of the Democratic Conference–from 1978 through 1988. He was re-elected to the Senate in 1968, 1974, 1980, 1986, and again in 1992.

Inouye is very popular in the Senate. His colleagues say he often works very quietly. He likes to compromise and he never grandstands, which might be why, when he does speak up, the other Senators listen.

Over the years, Inouye has served on the Senate Watergate Committee (1973-74), which investigated the charges that President Nixon and his administrative officials had engaged in, or conspired to cover up, a number of illegal activities in order to have President Nixon re-elected. In 1987, he was made chairman of the Senate Select Committee on Secret Military As-

> He became the first Japanese American ever to serve in Congress.

sistance to Iran and the Nicaraguan Opposition. The committee was formed in late 1986 to investigate reports that a group of Reagan administrative officials, using third-party countries and private citizens, had secretly sold weapons to Iran, and sent the profits to help the Nicaraguan Contras, which was in direct violation of President Reagan's declared policy and the expressed will of Congress.

One of the hottest topics to attract national attention in the 1990's was Clarence Thomas' nomination to the Supreme Court. The American Bar Association gave Clarence Thomas the lowest grade ever. He was not considered a good person for the Supreme Court, and several people thought he was judicially unfit. Inouye felt that Thomas was less than candid and he used reverse racism. "I'm sorry that my colleagues were afraid to stand up to him. They were reluctant because he was Black," Inouye has been quoted as saying. Clarence Thomas was eventually confirmed by the Senate and appointed to the Supreme Court. Thomas was known to be against women's rights to abortion, as was President Bush, who submitted Thomas for the Supreme Court nomination.

Mostly, Senator Inouye is a moderate, though his voting record in the Senate has consistently supported the liberals on such issues as abortion rights, school busing to achieve racial integration, and gun control. He often takes posi-

DANIEL KEN INOUYE

tions favorable to consumers and organized labor.

He is much more conservative when it comes to defense-related issues. He has often voted to increase military spending, particularly for research and development of sophisticated weapons. Even though he agrees that military spending should be cut in our upcoming budget, he still suggests caution in determining how large a reduction there should be in the military. Though he admits that the Cold War is over and we are not threatened by an invasion of the Soviet Union (the Russian Federation of Independent States), he still believes that we are threatened by other countries where there is the potential for upheaval and violence. He says that there is always uncertainty in this world and we need to be prepared to meet all threats. "Our democracy operates best when there is stability," says Inouye. "Often times, stability takes a little money, a little muscle." He currently approves of reducing our military forces by one-third over the next five years.

Inouye has recently become the chairman of the Select Committee on Indian Affairs, though he claims that he ended up on the committee because he was asked to look for a senator to fill a vacancy and he couldn't find a volunteer. "When I reported that to the Senate leader, he looked at me and said, 'Why don't you serve on the committee?' My response was, 'But Mr.

> "Our democracy operates best when there is stability," says Inouye. "Often times, stability takes a little money, a little muscle."

DANIEL KEN INOUYE

Leader, we don't have any Indian reservations on Hawaii.' His response was, 'At least you look like one!' Dan has taken his position very seriously and has investigated some of the atrocities committed by our government against the Native Americans. He believes that their affairs are a matter of national concern to all of us and he has worked hard to see that they receive fair treatment from the United States government.

In addition to his involvement in Native American affairs, Inouye is a member of the Committee on Rules and Administration, Chairman of the Democratic Steering Committee, Chairman of the Senate Appropriations subcommittee on Defense, and Chairman of the Senate Commerce, Science and Transportation subcommittee on Communications. A visitor to his office in the Hart Senate Office Building will find he has transferred a bit of Island cheerfulness to Washington. His office is decorated with Hawaiian carvings, paintings, and leis.

Inouye, though quite reserved by nature, is often in the middle of many Senate proceedings. His constant involvement often brings many calls and letters insulting his Japanese heritage. Inouye takes it all in stride. "It's part of life," he says. "If you can't take it, you've got no business around here. Racial discrimination will be with us for a long, long time and we should recognize the evil of it. I think most Americans do."

"Racial discrimination will be with us for a long, long time and we should recognize the evil of it. I think most Americans do."

DANIEL KEN INOUYE

My heroes are people you've never heard of.

Inouye has been quoted as saying that he prefers a good pool game to a congressional cocktail party. Actually, he loves fast food and reading. The stockily built senator is about five feet, six inches tall, with brown eyes, black hair, and a broad, friendly face. He is 69 years old, and still not thinking about retiring. His current Senate term does not expire until 1998, when he will be 74. He and his wife, Maggie, live in Bethesda, Maryland, where they built a four bedroom Pennsylvania Dutch style home nearly thirty years ago on a 30,000 square-foot lot that had once been part of a plant nursery. He still maintains a residence in Hawaii, where the Inouyes spend about two months a year. Maggie is involved with the Senate Wives Club, and often offers her comments on her husband's work-related plans and decisions. Their one son, Daniel Ken, Jr. (Kenny) was born in 1964, when Dan was forty years old. Inouye went to great lengths while Kenny was growing up, to make sure he had a life of his own, separate from his father's.

On the subject of heroes, Dan has been quoted as saying, "Throughout history, people have shown a craving for heroes who are larger than life, grand giants. My heroes are people you've never heard of. My father was a hero. He worked two jobs all his adult life, until he had his heart attack. His reward was to see his four children go to college–something that was denied him. You can repeat that story a thousand times throughout the United States. This is a country of heroes."

And there is no doubt that Dan Inouye is a hero, too. With his sedate manner and friendly attitude, Dan has worked to see that every American can enjoy a better life than his or her ancestors did before. His thirty-two years in the Senate have been marked by exceptional dedication to this country.

Inouye says of his years in Congress, "I hope I have rewarded my country at least in small part for the great rewards America has offered me."

Dan with wife, Maggie, and son, Dan, Jr.

YOSHIKO UCHIDA

Writer
1921-1992

66 **I** feel that children need the sense of continuity that comes through knowing about the past. All of us must understand our own past in order to move ahead into the future. I feel it's so important for Japanese American—and all Asian American—children to be aware of their history and culture, and to understand some of the traditions, feelings, and values of the early immigrants. At the same time, I write for all children, and I try to write about values and feelings that are universal. 99

Yoshiko Uchida

AS YOU READ

- Yoshiko Uchida feels that it is very important for all children to understand the history of their nation and their own culture. When you read the story, see if you can tell why she feels this is so important.

- Yoshiko's parents grew up in poverty in Japan. But here in the United States, they enjoyed a comfortable lifestyle. What provided these comforts?

- What event in United States history affected Yoshiko's life significantly? Do you think this same event affected the lives of other Japanese Americans?

YOSHIKO UCHIDA

On December 7, 1941, Yoshiko had been studying for her final exams at the University of California at Berkeley. While she was at the library, the FBI came to her house twice. No one was home. Her parents and sister had gone out to visit friends, not aware of how serious the Japanese attack on Pearl Harbor had been. The FBI were very concerned that no one was to be found, so they broke into the Uchida home without a warrant. They were looking for Dwight Takashi Uchida, Yoshiko's father, who was a prominent Japanese American businessman. When her father returned home, he saw that someone had broken in, and believing that he had been burglarized, called the police. Two policemen and three FBI men appeared. Two of the FBI agents asked Mr. Uchida to come with them for questioning. Dwight Uchida went willingly. The remaining FBI agent stayed with her mother and sister to intercept any phone calls and to make sure that they did not contact anyone. One policeman guarded the front door, and one positioned himself at the back door, essentially holding them prisoners in their own home.

When Yoshiko returned home from the library, she found that her father had been taken by the FBI to the San Francisco Immigration Headquarters. She found her mother thoughtfully serving tea to the FBI agent who had remained. But Yoshiko could not be so gracious to the man who had taken her father away, and

> One policeman guarded the front door, and one positioned himself at the back door, essentially holding them prisoners in their own home.

she stormed off to her room, slamming her door behind her. Little did she understand that this incident was only the beginning of the years of imprisonment that all Japanese Americans living on the west coast would face.

Yoshiko Uchida was born on November 24, 1921 in Alameda, California to Dwight Takashi Uchida and Iku (Umegaki) Uchida. She was the younger of two daughters. She had a sister named Keiko.

Yoshiko's father, Dwight Uchida (back row) with his mother (center front) and four sisters. Japan about 1902.

> Because her father was well educated and held a good paying job as an executive..., Yoshiko and Keiko grew up with all the amenities that other American children knew.

YOSHIKO UCHIDA

Dwight Uchida was a first generation immigrant (issei), who had grown up in poverty in Japan. His father had died when he was ten, and his mother sent her five children off to live with various relatives. An uncle raised Dwight. He worked his way through Doshisha University in Kyoto by delivering milk in the mornings, working as a telephone operator at night, and later serving as a clerk in a bank. He came to California in 1906, when he was twenty-two years old. He had hoped to go to Yale to become a doctor, but he abandoned these ambitions when he found he enjoyed business. In 1916, Iku Umegaki, Yoshiko's mother left Japan and sailed to a strange land to marry Uchida, whom she had only met through correspondence. Iku had also been educated at Doshisha University (1914) although it was some years after Dwight had attended. She was twenty-four years old when she left her family in Japan and came to the United States to marry a man that her professors at Doshisha University had recommended. The arranged marriage proved successful and the Uchidas had two children. Because her father was well educated and held a good paying job as an executive at Matsui (a now defunct Japanese Corporation), Yoshiko and Keiko grew up with all the amenities that other American children knew. The family enjoyed many more comforts than most other Japanese American families in the early part of the twentieth century. Japanese immigrants could not become citizens nor own land at this time.

YOSHIKO UCHIDA

The Uchidas rented a pretty three-bedroom stucco bungalow on Stuart Street in Berkeley. There were peach, apricot, and fig trees in the back yard. Dwight Uchida loved to garden and Yoshiko remembered there were sweetpeas that grew bigger than she was and chrysanthemums that measured seventeen inches around!

The house on Stuart Street.

But, despite the happy home, Yoshiko felt different in the outside world. She wanted to be like everyone else. She wanted to be viewed as an American. "When people saw me," she wrote, "they usually saw only my Japanese face." The prejudice and discrimination she faced was often open and hostile and hurt Yoshiko very much. One day a stranger on the street shouted, "Go back where you came from!" But Yoshiko was born in the United States and this was where she came from. Often, she and her sister were not invited to parties or other social events given by their white classmates. Yoshiko was made to feel different and foreign in her homeland.

Her mother and father made her feel safe and secure at home. The Japanese culture, values, and traditions were an integral part of their lives. Though the family had a predominantly Western outlook and lifestyle, the dominant language in their home was Japanese. All of Mr. Uchida's business was conducted in English, however, and Keiko and Yoshiko spoke English in school and to each other. Because their mother and father had known poverty early in life, they were very generous to others and very compassionate to anyone in need. When one of their neighbors on Stuart Street lost his job during the depression, and his wife sold homemade bread to try to make ends meet, Iku not only bought her bread to help her out, she arranged to take French lessons from her as well, to give her some additional income.

The Uchidas opened their home to many lonely students from Japan studying at the University of California. The students were always present on holidays, most Sundays, and they often dropped by uninvited. Yoshiko and Keiko did not always treat their house guests with the utmost respect and they often found them dull. But when Yoshiko looked back on these gatherings years later, she remembered the smell of sukiyaki and the after-dinner singing around the piano, and she realized she actually had enjoyed these times. Of course, the students were not the only guests in the Uchida home. There were visiting ministers, alumni from Doshisha University, and sometimes the president of the university would drop by himself!

Yoshiko described her mother as a giving and deeply caring person. She would tell her daughters stories from Japan. She loved to read and the house was filled with books. Her mother was also creative and liked to write; she often wrote poems on scraps of paper. Her main devotion, however, was to her family. Yoshiko learned her love of reading and writing from her mother. "It seems to me I've been interested in books and writing for as long as I can remember," wrote Yoshiko. "I was writing stories when I was ten, and being the child of frugal immigrant parents, I wrote them on brown wrapping paper which I cut up and bound into booklets... The first is titled, 'Jimmy Chipmonk and His Friends: A Short Story for Small Children.'" She also kept a journal where she recorded all the significant events in her life.

Dwight Uchida had a railroad pass that enabled the family to take many trips. Often, Mr. Uchida combined his business trips with family trips. One summer when she was ten, Yoshiko and her family took a trip across the country to Connecticut. "We visited several eastern cities,"

Yoshiko Uchida

she recalled, "but most important to my mother was a special trip we made to the small village of Cornwall, Connecticut, to visit one of her former Doshisha instructors...and to meet for the first time two white women pen pals with whom she had corresponded since college. Both my mother and father were great letter writers and kept up voluminous correspondence. They cherished their many friends and I don't believe

Yoshiko, about 3 years old, with Keiko, about 7

either of them ever lost one for neglect on their part.

Yoshiko Uchida

"We were probably the first Asians ever to visit Cornwall and one of its residents, an elderly white woman, patted me on the head and said, 'My, but you speak English so beautifully.' She had looked at my Japanese face and addressed only my outer person, and although she had meant to compliment me, I was thoroughly abashed to be perceived as a foreigner..."

It was numerous incidents like this one that taught Yoshiko to be quiet and cautious to the outside world. The rejection she experienced so often affected her sense of personal worth and reinforced her own feelings of inferiority. Many times she was accepted by her friends as an equal, and then an incident would occur that would remind her that she was not quite perceived as "equal." When Yoshiko was in junior high school, she was the only Japanese American to join the Girl Reserve unit at school. All the other girls treated her the same as everyone else and Yoshiko had fun with this activity. One day, the unit was to be photographed for the local newspaper. The photographer kept casually trying to ease Yoshiko out of the picture, but one of her friends kept insisting she be in it.

In elementary school, Yoshiko remembered being singled out by her teachers for her excellent grades. But, by the time she was in high school, she remembered being singled out by the other white students and excluded from all their activities. She was so unhappy in high school

> "We were probably the first Asians ever to visit Cornwall and one of its residents, an elderly white woman, patted me on the head and said, 'My, but you speak English so beautifully.'"

that she couldn't wait to get out. She increased her class load, and graduated in two and a half years. She entered the University of California when she was only sixteen. But, college was even worse than high school. Asian Americans were not invited to join sororities or fraternities, which in the late 1930's was an integral part of campus life. There were two Japanese American social clubs on campus, the Japanese Women's Student Club and the Japanese Men's Student Club. They had their own dances, picnics, and special events, and these became the only social events that Yoshiko could participate in.

"For many years I never spoke to a white person unless he or she spoke to me first," recalled Yoshiko. "At one of my freshman classes at the university, I found myself sitting next to a white student I had known slightly in high school. I sat silent and tense, not even turning to look at her because I didn't want to speak first and be rebuffed. Finally, she turned to me and said, 'Yoshi, aren't you going to speak to me?'"

All during her college years, Yoshiko dated only nisei (second generation Japanese American). All of her girlfriends were almost exclusively nisei, too. Though she had always wanted to be accepted as an American, she felt most comfortable in the company of other Japanese Americans. "We nisei were, in effect, rejected as inferior Americans by our own country and rejected as inferior by the country of our parents as well. We were neither totally American nor totally Japanese, but a unique fusion of the two..."

One of the many Uchida family portraits taken when Yoshiko's grandmother came to visit from Los Angeles.

Yoshiko Uchida

Then came the bombing of Pearl Harbor, Hawaii, and Yoshiko found her life completely uprooted and disrupted. Her mother and father were classified as enemy aliens and Mr. Uchida was sent to a prisoner-of-war camp in Missoula, Montana. The government blocked their bank accounts, and there was total confusion as to what the family could withdraw for living expenses. Since Dwight Uchida could no longer work, there was no more income. On February 19, 1942, President Franklin D. Roosevelt signed executive order 9066 that relocated all Japanese Americans living on the west coast. Even before this order was signed, the FBI had imprisoned nearly all the first-generation Japanese Americans, which were most of the leaders in the community. The young nisei from the Japanese American Citizens League met in an emergency session to try to decide how to best handle the intolerable situation and unprecedented act of our government. Not wanting bloodshed or violence, the JACL leaders decided that the community should cooperate with the government under protest.

On April 21, 1942, removal orders were issued for the Uchida family as well as all other Japanese Americans living in the Berkeley area. They were given ten days to dispose of their homes and personal possessions. The Uchidas lost nearly everything they had. By May 1, Yoshiko and her family were imprisoned in the Tanforan Racetrack. Dwight Uchida was even-

Yoshiko Uchida

tually released from the camp in Montana and allowed to join his family in Tanforan. The family lived for the next five months in a ten-foot by twenty-foot horse stall. The entire camp was surrounded by barbed wire. "Dust, dirt, and wood shavings covered the linoleum that had been laid over manure-covered boards, the smell of horses hung in the air, and the whitened corpses of many insects still clung to the hastily white-washed walls...Living in our stable were an assortment of people–mostly small family units–that included an artist, my father's barber and his wife, a dentist and his wife, a group of Kibei bachelors (Japanese born in the United States, but educated in Japan), an insurance salesman and his wife, and a widow with two daughters..." Yoshiko wrote. The Japanese Americans organized schools, churches, and recreation areas. Yoshiko taught second grade and decided she might like to teach later on. She and other Japanese American classmates had missed their graduation by two weeks, and her diploma was sent to her in the mail at the internment camp.

By September 1942, the Uchidas and others were sent to Topaz, a camp in the Utah desert. Dust storms were so severe that the families could not keep their barracks or clothes clean. The weather was so harsh and changeable that the interns were constantly ill. Yoshiko's experiences along with those of other Japanese Americans in the internment camps during World

On April 21, 1942, removal orders were issued for the Uchida family as well as all other Japanese Americans living in the Berkeley area. They were given ten days to dispose of their homes and possessions.

YOSHIKO UCHIDA

War II were later retold in her books, *Journey to Topaz* (1971) and *Journey Home*, (1978) which she wrote for children. *Journey to Topaz* tells the story of twelve-year-old Yuki, a second-generation Japanese American girl in Berkeley, California, and what happens to her family after the bombing of Pearl Harbor. The story follows Yuki and her family to an internment camp in the Utah desert. In *Journey Home*, Yuki and her family return to California after the war to rebuild their lives. She also wrote *Desert Exile: The Uprooting of a Japanese American Family* (1982) for adults, which chronicled much of her life through World War II.

Yoshiko waited a long time to write these stories about the Japanese American experience during World War II. She was afraid that before the late 1960's, most people were not ready to listen to the story of the Japanese Americans. She was afraid that no publisher would accept it. But later, there was a greater acceptance of the events of this time, and Yoshiko felt she had to write these books to make sure that such events would never again be repeated in United States history. In the 1970's and 80's, she often got questions from third-generation Japanese Americans as to why the issei and nisei did not rebel against the World War II internment. She wanted them to understand that the world was a very different place in 1942 and at that time, most Japanese felt that the only way to demon-

Yoshiko waited a long time to write these stories about the Japanese American experience during World War II.

strate their loyalty to the United States was to cooperate with the government.

Yoshiko did manage to leave Topaz in May 1943 with the help of the Student Relocation Committee. She obtained a fellowship to do graduate work at Smith College in Northampton, Massachussetts. The Student Relocation Committee eventually helped over three thousand students leave the internment camps to enter some five hundred institutions of higher education throughout the country.

"I left Topaz determined to work hard and prove I was as loyal as any other American. I felt a tremendous sense of responsibility to make good, not just for myself, but for all Japanese Americans," she said. Yoshiko received her master's in education from Smith College in 1944.

Unfortunately, Dwight and Iku Uchida were not permitted to leave Topaz until the end of the war. When they did, Dwight Uchida had no job to return to and the family had no home. Work for issei after the war was difficult to come by. For many years, Mr. Uchida attempted work as an unskilled laborer, never lasting long in any one job. It was ten years before they were able to buy a home again, this time with the help of their daughter, Keiko.

Yoshiko taught in a small Quaker school in Philadelphia, Pennsylvania for a year after she

> "I left Topaz determined to work hard and prove I was as loyal as any other American."

YOSHIKO UCHIDA

graduated from Smith, but she found she had no time for her writing. So she and her family moved to New York City and she took a nine-to-five job as a secretary. Her parents eventually returned to California to try to rebuild their lives. In 1952, she was awarded a fellowship to study in Japan and she spent two years as a Ford Foundation Foreign Area Fellow. In Japan, she met friends and relatives that she had never seen in person. Though she went primarily as a writer to collect more Japanese Folktales, she came home aware of a new dimension to herself as a Japanese American.

When she returned to America, she wrote many books for children. She published three collections of Japanese Folktales and numerous stories about Japanese children and their experiences. Beginning in 1970, Yoshiko wrote about her experiences as a Japanese American. *A Jar of Dreams*, published by Atheneum in 1982, is typical of Yoshiko's many books for young adults. She tells the story of Rinko, an eleven-year-old Japanese American girl made to feel different and left out, and not as good as her classmates. The story takes place during the Depression when Aunt Waka arrives from Japan for the summer. It is Aunt Waka that helps each family member discover their inner strengths and by summer's end, Rinko knows how special her Aunt Waka is. Two very popular books were published as sequels: *The Best Bad Thing* (1983) and *The Happiest Ending* (1985).

YOSHIKO UCHIDA

Yoshiko traveled extensively in the United States and abroad. She lectured at conferences on children's literature and participated in many programs for Japanese Americans. She wrote and published 27 books for children from 1949 to 1991 for which she won many awards and honors.

"Although all my books have been about Japanese people, my hope is that they will enlarge and enrich the reader's understanding, not only of the Japanese and the Japanese Americans, but of the *human condition*. I think it's important for each of us to take pride in our special heritage, but we must never lose our sense of connection with the community of man. And I hope our young people will, through the enriching diversity of the books they read, learn to celebrate our common humanity and the universality of the human spirit."

In June 1992, Yoshiko Uchida died from a stroke at the Alta Bates Medical Center in Berkeley, California. She was seventy years old.

"I think it's important for each of us to take pride in our special heritage, but we must never lose our sense of connection with the community of man."

HAING NGOR

1947-
Doctor, actor, author

"I have been many things in life: A trader walking barefoot on paths through the jungles. A medical doctor driving to his clinic in a shiny Mercedes...to the surprise of many people, and above all myself, I have been a Hollywood actor. But nothing has shaped my life as much as surviving the Pol Pot regime. I am a survivor of the Cambodian holocaust. That's who I am. **"**

Haing Ngor, Excerpt from *A Cambodian Odyssey*, Macmillan, 1987

AS YOU READ

- The torture and misery inflicted on the people of Cambodia is something that most Americans never experience in their lifetime. As you read the story, think about our freedom in the United States. Where would you rather live?

- As you read the story, see if you can surmise what situations might have led to the constant war in Southeast Asia.

- When you read, you will see that Haing Ngor did not have the same opportunities for an education in Cambodia that we have in the United States. Why do you think Haing struggled against his parent's wishes to continue his education?

- Most of us in the United States have plenty to eat every day. For years, there was always enough to eat in Cambodia. See if you can determine from the story what might have caused the shortage of food, and why so many people became sick and died of starvation.

HAING NGOR

For many years, Cambodia struggled in civil war as opposing factions vied for control of the region. For four years, the country was controlled by the brutal, communist Khmer Rouge regime. The citizens were beaten and tortured. Everything they owned was taken from them. There was no food and sickness took the lives of as many Cambodians as did the government soldiers themselves. There were no medical supplies, no medicine, no shelter, and nothing to eat. There was only terror as each afternoon, the soldiers came into the fields to take prisoners. Maybe one day they would take away six men. Maybe three the next. No one ever knew why...but most of them never came back.

One day, the soldiers came for Haing. They tied him up with rope and led him through the woods to a collection of buildings in a clearing. A prison guard then led him to a large grove of mango trees, where prisoners sat at the base of each tree, tied to the trunk. All had been brutalized, all were in pain. The guard tied Haing to a mango tree as Haing began to pray.

Red ants crawled all over his body and bit his scalp, his shoulders, and his chest. He could not move to swat them away. As darkness fell over the prison camp, a big man, carrying a hatchet came to Haing to ask if he was Vietnamese or Chinese. Then the guard wanted to know what occupation Haing had been engaged

> One day, the soldiers came for Haing. They tied him up with rope...Red ants crawled all over his body...

in before the Khmer Rouge regime took over. Haing could not tell them he had been a doctor, because the regime was killing all the doctors. The regime saw no need for any doctors. Haing told the guard he had been a taxi driver. "I can tell you are lying," roared the guard.

The guard called for help. Another man came to help tighten the ropes around Haing. They pushed him over on his side. While the second man held his neck down in the dirt, the first one put Haing's hand on top of a tree root, and then stepped on his wrist with his foot. Then he swung his hatchet and chopped off the tip of Haing's finger. "Why don't we cut off a toe?" asked the second man. "We shouldn't let him walk." Then they hacked off part of his ankle with an axe. Haing did not die, so the guards let him go.

Cambodia had not always been like this. The traditional, peaceful Cambodian way of life was lost in 1975, when Pol Pot (known as Saloth Sar before the revolution) and his Khmer Rouge communists assumed control.

Born in 1947 in the village of Samrong Yong, just south of the Cambodian capital of Phnom Penh, Haing S. Ngor was the third child born to Kea Ngor and Lim Ngor. He had two older brothers, a younger brother, and three younger sisters. Haing's father was a descendant of the

HAING NGOR

Chinese. Most Cambodians are descendants of the Khmer race. Haing is a mixture of Chinese and Khmer. There are other residents of Vietnam ancestry or other mixed races.

Cambodia is a part of Indochina, located in southeast Asia. It is about the size of the state of Washington, or about one-third the size of France. For many years, the region was known as French Indochina because France colonized Cambodia and the neighboring countries of Laos and Vietnam beginning in the mid-nineteenth century. French and Khmer are the dominant languages in Cambodia, though Khmer is the official language of the dominant, dark-skinned Khmer race. The French-backed government was very corrupt, which led to much dissatisfaction. Government officials would kidnap wealthy citizens for ransom, or would demand bribe money in exchange for peaceful passage to the market. Haing's father was a very wealthy and prosperous man in the days before the communists took over. Consequently, he was often kidnapped, and Haing's mother would have to raise the money for his release. Though it was an intolerable situation from an American point of view, it was nothing compared to the terror that was to follow years later.

In 1953, France recognized Cambodia's independence, and in 1955, King Norodom Sihanouk gave up the throne. Sihanouk became prime minister in 1955 and head of state in 1960. From

Haing Ngor

1955 to 1963, Cambodia received millions of dollars in aid from the United States, but in 1963, Sihanouk cut off all U.S. aid. He charged that the United States was supporting attempts to overthrow the government of Cambodia.

Before the Khmer Rouge communists took over in 1975, Haing remembers a relatively peaceful way of life. There were always occasional gunshots, but there really was no mass destruction to speak of. His mother and father owned a dry goods store and later a trucking business and a lumber mill. Though his parents were often well-off, the government kept taking most of their money in bribes or ransom. Haing and his older brother, Pheng Huor, were sent to a private Chinese school. But soon, Kea could not afford tuition for both boys, and Haing had to quit and help with the business. When Sihanouk became the sovereign leader, he increased the number of free public schools. Haing entered primary school with other twelve- to fourteen-year-olds just learning how to read, like him. In his first year, he was able to pass four grades. The next year, he passed two more. From there he went to a public secondary school in the provincial capital of Takeo. Most classes in school were conducted in French which still culturally dominated the small Cambodian society that was educated or rich. Haing continued to do well in school. He passed the exam that allowed him to go on to high school.

Though his parents were often well-off, the government kept taking most of their money in bribes or ransom.

HAING NGOR

At this point, by Buddhist custom, Haing became a monk. He shaved his head and eyebrows. His parents saluted him, and each morning, he walked barefoot in a line of monks, silently chanting prayers. He spent his days doing chores around the temple and in prayer. A wrinkled old monk made sure that Haing understood the essential teachings of Buddha. "What is holy and divine," the monk explained, "is life itself, as it runs through your family. You must understand this clearly. It takes a father and a mother to bring a child into the world. They protect him when he is young. It is the duty of the child to protect them when they grow old. You must also honor all the children of the family who came into the world ahead of you. You must always serve and protect them. Obey your elders, boy. If all the families are happy, then the village will be happy. If all the villages are happy, then the land will be strong and content."

> "...If all the families are happy, then the village will be happy. If all the villages are happy, then the land will be strong and content."

But this was not to be. As Haing later told us, his family was unhappy, his village was unhappy, and so was his country. And as such, this led to a terrible revolution many years later.

Kea Ngor could not read or write Khmer, though he spoke it fluently. Pheng Huor, Haing's older brother, could read and write a little Khmer, but not well. Neither father nor son spoke French. Most government documents were in Khmer and French and it was Haing's duty to help with this paperwork. In 1968, Haing had failed an exam that would have allowed him to continue on at the university. His father wanted him to quit school and work full time in the family business. But Haing wanted to be a doctor, and he retook the courses, and the exam. He went on to study medicine at the national university. In the rural areas of Cambodia, most health care is provided by spirit doctors, who interpret dreams, cast spells, and use magic, and by herbalists who make medicines from plants. But this type of medicine could not help infection and had no method of surgery. There were only a few doctors trained in Western medicine and many more were needed. Haing decided to study obstetrics and gynecology because the field of women's health was particularly backward in Cambodia. More than fifty-percent of the babies born in Cambodia died.

All of his courses were conducted in French. Because there was such a shortage of doctors in Cambodia, students were permitted to practice before they got their degrees. In the meantime, Haing decided to teach remedial science part-time for money to get through college. In addition, he tutored in private homes.

A friend of Haing's at the university had two younger sisters who were having difficulty with their studies. Haing was hired to tutor these two young girls, the Kam sisters, and their cousin, named Huoy Chang. The girls all passed the courses for which Haing had tutored them. From this relationship, Haing and Huoy developed a lasting friendship, and though they were prevented from having a traditional wedding, first by Haing's father who wanted Haing to marry a rich girl, and later by the revolution, they declared themselves to be husband and wife, hoping that someday in the future they could have their traditional wedding. Huoy and her mother, Ma, had lived alone nearly all their lives. Huoy's father had been killed by a burglar shortly after Huoy was born.

By March of 1970, Cambodia was still relatively at peace. But all around them was war. To the east, South Vietnam, North Vietnam, and the United States were at war. To the north, Laos was involved in a similar war between the communists and the royalists. Cambodia was stuck in the middle. Life went on as usual. In the capital of Phnom Penh, the merchants bustled in the market and enjoyed long lunchtime siestas. In the surrounding countryside, the monks made their silent rounds collecting alms. In the middle of the day, the farmers came home from the fields. At night, one could hear the sounds of homemade instruments throughout the tiny villages.

But trouble began on March 11, 1970, when Prince Norodom Sihanouk was out of the country. Sihanouk was ousted by his prime minister, General Lon Nol. The North Vietnamese invaded Cambodia and riots broke out everywhere. Sihanouk then joined forces with his former enemies, the Cambodian communists, even though he had persecuted them for years. He had nicknamed them the red Khmers, or in French, Khmers Rouge. He set up a "government in exile." Because Sihanouk had been so well liked by his country, he was able to give some credibility to the communist forces he had joined. Many Cambodians, particularly those from the rural areas, worshipped Sihanouk and would do anything he asked. But at this time, there were only a few thousand Khmer Rouge and the real threat was coming from the North Vietnamese, who then overran about a third of the country. As the Khmer Rouge grew in strength, however, they began to replace the North Vietnamese in fighting the Lon Nol regime.

Many citizens were forced to leave their villages as the communists took over. In late 1972, Haing and his family had to leave their home and their lumber mill in the little village of Samrong Yong. The family moved to Phnom Penh along with many, many other people.

The war continued. The United States started some bombing missions over Cambodia, but stopped in 1973, supplying only weapons and advisers to the Lon Nol government. By 1973, the Khmer Rouge had assumed all the fighting from the North Vietnamese. The government fought back, but each day, the country was

In late 1972, Haing and his family had to leave their home and their lumber mill in the little village of Samrong Yong.

squeezed in a little closer. Roads were cut off. Many merchants sent their possessions and their daughters out of the country. But those who stayed thought the fighting would soon be over.

In February 1975, Haing Ngor was awarded a medical degree and became a full-fledged doctor. On April 12, 1975, the Americans evacuated Phnom Penh in helicopters. Over the loudspeakers, the new leaders told all the citizens to leave the cities and move to the rural areas to work as farmers. "The Red Flag of Revolution is Flying Over Liberated Phnom Penh," came one of the communist slogans. The new communist regime required everyone to dress alike and discouraged the practice of religion. The new government took control of all the businesses and farms.

On April 17, footsteps sounded in the corridor of the hospital where Haing was working. He was in the middle of a difficult operation, and his patient, a young soldier that had been wounded in the war, lay unconscious on the operating table with a large incision down his belly. The operating room doors burst open. There stood a communist guerilla in black shirt and trousers, and black rubber sandals made from automobile tires. Another guerilla burst in armed with a Chinese-made AK-47. He put the barrel to Haing's head. "You the doctor?" he demanded.

> The new communist regime required everyone to dress alike and discouraged the practice of religion. The new government took control of all the businesses and farms.

"No," lied Haing, "the doctor just left. You missed him." The guerillas took off after the imaginary doctor but threatened to come back and kill Haing if they did not find the real doctor outside. Haing knew he had only moments to escape with his life. All the nurses were screaming hysterically. "Okay," Haing said, "Everybody go." Sadly, Haing had to leave the wounded soldier to die on the operating table, a vision that has haunted him ever since.

Outside, guerillas in ragged uniforms swarmed all over the city. Thousands of people filled the streets. Car horns were blaring. There was an occasional gunshot. White sheets hung from the buildings in surrender as Phnom Penh gave in to the Khmer Rouge. For several days, Haing walked eastward. Here and there, corpses lay on the road. Eventually, he reached the edge of a crowded settlement of refugees in an enormous temple compound on the Mekong River. People were camping everywhere. They had nowhere else to go. Haing decided to stay there, too, roaming around everyday looking for his parents, his brothers and sisters, and his wife and her mother.

After many days, Haing found his mother, father, his brothers and their wives. They were living under a tarp tied between some trees. He continued to search for his wife, whom he found safe with her mother several days later. He brought them all together. But every day, the

HAING NGOR

Khmer Rouge announced on the loudspeaker that everyone must go to the countryside. If they did not go voluntarily to work the fields, the Khmer Rouge would pick a location for them. Huoy, Ma, and Haing decided to go to the Chang's home province of Kampot, along the Gulf of Siam in an attempt to flee to safety in Thailand. His father wanted to go in the other direction, and so the family was separated.

Haing, Ma, and Huoy had walked for only a few hours when they were stopped by some Khmer Rouge soldiers, children no more than ten years old! They were told they could go no further and had to stop right there and go to work. They led them to a village near the edge of the jungle and ordered them to hammer rocks into gravel.

> The Khmer Rouge continued to kill hundreds of thousands of citizens and former government officials.

The Khmer Rouge continued to kill hundreds of thousands of citizens and former government officials. They killed educated people and people who were not strong enough to do the work required by the government. Haing, Huoy and Ma decided again to try to escape, this time to join Haing's parents in Tonle Bati, where they had been headed. They crept out at night. But by the time they arrived in mid-1975, they found the Khmer Rouge had taken over there, too. They had forced all the monks out of the temple and made them wear black pajamas. They closed the schools, claiming no need for education. They said no one needed engineers or doctors!

One day the Khmer Rouge said they wanted everyone to return to their native villages. Haing again began to think of plans for the family's escape to Thailand. But it was not to be. They headed to Battambang Province, which had been a fertile rice bowl for the country before the war. On the way, Ma fell into the river and drowned, much to Huoy and Haing's dismay.

When they arrived, they were told to choose land in the village of Phum Chhleav and build a house. The rice fields had been long neglected, and there was no food in the area. Huoy and Haing began to look for wild food to eat. They looked for red ants, which the rural Cambodians often put in soup to add a crunchy texture. They looked for lizards and edible plants. All the while, they had to watch for the government soldiers who would shoot anyone they saw scrounging for food. The people became very malnourished and sick. Many, many died.

In the next years, Haing was taken prisoner and tortured and brutalized on three separate occasions. For some reason, he never died like the rest of them. Huoy and Haing became separated from the rest of the family when they had been moved to the front lines farther south. His brother's children were taken and sent to a youth camp to be brainwashed into forgetting their parents and to become soldiers for the government. His mother was sent off to work in the jungles and was never heard from again. His father was arrested, held captive, and then killed for stealing food. Two weeks later, his brother and his wife were taken away with their hands tied. They never came back.

But Huoy and Haing never gave up hope. The killings went on, but Haing continued to find a reason to live. He built a house for the two of them and planted a garden. One day, Haing met a man named Som, whom he had known when he had been a doctor at the military hospital. Som had been an interpreter at the U.S. embassy in Phnom Penh. Sometimes, when no one was around, Som spoke English for Haing and it sounded just like the Voice of America on the radio broadcasts. Haing began to dream of going to America. "I'd rather be a dog in America," Haing told Huoy, "than be a human being in Cambodia." Huoy said she would be happy if she could just have a house with plenty to eat and lots of babies. Haing still wished to be a dog in America.

In late 1977, things seemed to be going much better for Haing and Huoy. They were happy and healthy. Then there was joyous news: Huoy was pregnant! But soon, the dry season came, and the food was in short supply. By April 1978, the common kitchen closed and the people were

> "I'd rather be a dog in America," Haing told Huoy, "than be a human being in Cambodia."

again left to find food on their own. The food was not yet ready in their garden. By the time Huoy was in her fifth month of pregnancy, there was little left to eat. The weather continued to be very hot and dry. At seven months, Huoy went into premature labor. There were no surgical instruments to help Huoy or the baby. There was no food for Huoy or the baby. Haing tried desperately to get permission to take Huoy to the old government hospital in Battambang City. When he went to the Khmer Rouge headquarters to ask permission to send Huoy on a train to Battambang, the soldiers laughed at him. Panicked as the hours slipped away, Haing could do nothing but watch Huoy die.

Huoy died on June 2, 1978, and soon after, the rains came. Then there was food again to eat, but it was too late for Huoy. Haing was left all alone. In the day, he worked, never caring if the soldiers took him as a prisoner. At night he visited Huoy's grave.

Soon, Haing heard that the North Vietnamese were invading Cambodia. He was actually happy that the Vietnamese had come because Haing could not imagine anything more brutal than the regime of Khmer Rouge.

In early January 1979, a freight train arrived in Phnom Penh. Khmer Rouge soldiers sat in the boxcars. A few days later long lines of civilians began to arrive from the south. Every

HAING NGOR

day people were tied up and led away at gun-point. They never returned. With one wrong glance, entire families were executed. Certainly things had gotten no better.

Haing prepared for a quick getaway. He told his remaining relatives and their wives and children to get prepared if they wanted to go to the Thai border. Amid the chattering of automatic rifles, Haing moved on, first north to the national highway, and from there, west to Thailand. He walked along ox-cart trails, through rice fields, and through jungles. In May 1979, Haing escaped from Cambodia, which was then being "liberated" from the Khmer Rouge by Vietnam! As the sun was sinking, Haing looked around at all the tents and makeshift huts just over the Thai border. He was surprised by how many had escaped before him. But of the forty-one people in Haing's immediate family, including his parents, brothers and sisters and their spouses and children, plus Huoy, her mother, and Haing, only nine survived this far.

On August 30, 1980, Haing finally managed to leave Thailand for the United States. He was finally free. Even though he arrived with only four dollars to his name, he was finally free.

"In America," Haing wrote, "it never occurred to me that my life was in any danger or that there was any risk of starvation. I wasn't worried about having only four dollars."

> With one glance, entire families were executed.

His first job was as a night security guard for a company outside of Chinatown. He took lessons in English at Evans Community College.

In November 1980, he became a caseworker for the Chinatown Service Center. His office provided free job placement services to the refugees. Most of the refugees had to start all over again, and rebuild their lives in America. The refugees had to adapt to a culture that was very different from their own. For years and years, the Cambodians had followed their own customs until the Communists put an end to their way of life. They lost everything–their families, the monks, their villages, their land, and all their possessions. When they came to the United States, they could not put their old life back together. They had to make an entirely new life in a strange land, but at least there was peace and plenty to eat.

In the 1984 film, *The Killing Fields*, Haing Ngor was cast in the role of Dith Pran, a Cambodian reporter, whose experiences with the Khmer Rouge closely paralleled his own. The story was about Sydney Schanberg, a New York Times correspondent in Cambodia during the Lon Nol years. Schanberg did not speak Khmer or know much about Cambodian culture, and he needed Dith Pran to be his eyes and ears. He depended on Pran when they ran into obstacles or situations that threatened their lives. For almost four years, while the Khmer Rouge

HAING NGOR

ruled Cambodia, Schanberg heard nothing from Dith Pran. Finally, when Vietnam invaded Cambodia, Pran escaped to Thailand, where he met Schanberg again.

Haing Ngor became a U.S. citizen in 1986.

For his performance in this Hollywood film, Haing was awarded an Oscar for the best supporting actor. In 1987, he published his autobiography, *A Cambodian Odyssey* (Macmillan).

As you can see, Haing Ngor was able to build a brand new life in the United States. Within seven years in this country, he starred in a major movie and published a book, accomplishments that few of us can claim in a lifetime!

aggressive *adj.* (a-gres-siv) assertive, outgoing, pushy, ready to do battle

ancestry *n.* (an-ses-tree) persons who are included in line of descent

amputate *vb.* (am-pyou-tayt) to cut off

appellate *adj.* (a-pel-it) of, or relating to appeals; to look at again

articulate *adj.* (ar-tik-you-lit) able to get ideas across well in speech

assurance *n.* (a-shur-ents) a guarantee

astonish *vb.* (e-ston-ish) strike with fear, wonder, or surprise

colleague *n.* (koll-eeg) an associate in a profession

compromise *n., vb.* (kom-pre-myz) settlement by mutual concession; to come to an agreement by mutual concession

conservative *adj. n.* (kun-ser-vi-tiv) traditional; tending to maintain existing views; marked by moderation; a person with these traits

constraint *n.* (kun-straynt) the state of being constricted and restrained

controversial *adj.* (kon-troh-ver-shel) of or pertaining to something that many people disagree about

critical *adj.* (krit-i-kal) exercise careful judgment; to judge harshly

culture *n.* (kul-cher) the beliefs, social forms, habits, and traditions of a racial, religious, or social group of people

custom *n.* (kus-tem) a long-established practice considered as an unwritten law

debut *vb.* (day-byou) a first appearance

delegate *n.* (del-i-get) a representative of a U.S. territory in the House of Representatives; a member of a lower house, such as the state legislature

delude *vb.* (de-lood) to mislead, trick, or deceive

deter *vb.* (dee-ter) stop

detonate *vb.* (de-ti-nate) to set off an explosion

devotion *n.* (de-voh-shun) the state of being dedicated and loyal

disclose *vb.* (dis-kloz) to reveal or show

distinguish *vb.* (dis-ting-wish) to single out; to show a difference

disqualify *vb.* (dis-qwal-i-fy) to make not qualified; not eligible

emigrate *vb.* (em-i-grayt) to leave one's place of residence or country and live elsewhere

ethics *n.* (eth-iks) a set of moral principles or values

grandstand *vb.* (grand-stand) to act so as to impress onlookers; for attention

heritage *n.* (her-a-tij) something transmitted or acquired from a predecessor; family legacy; tradition

humiliate *vb.* (hyou-mil-i-ate) to reduce to a lower position in one's own view

immigrant *n.* (im-i-grent) a person that comes to a country to take up permanent residence

inadequate *adj.* (in-ad-i-kwet) insufficient; not adequate

GLOSSARY

inclination *n*. (in-kli-nay-shun) a natural disposition toward; to be inclined toward

induce *vb*. (in-doos) to cause

inferior *adj*. (in-fear-i-er) not as good as

intimidate *vb*. (in-tim-i-dayt) to frighten

liberal *n*. (lib-ral) one who is open-minded and not strict

migrate *vb*. (my-grayt) to move from one country to another

moderate *adj*. (mo-der-et) avoiding extremes; calm

naturalized citizen *n*. one whose birthplace is not in the country to which he or she later pledges loyalty; one who becomes a citizen by applying to the government of a country where one was not born

nisei *n*. (nee-sayee) second-generation Japanese-American; born in the United States to parents of Japanese descent

nominate *vb*. (nom-i-nayt) to designate, or name

oppress *vb*. (a-press) to crush

precedent *n*. (press-i-dent) something that was done previously that sets an example for subsequent acts to follow

prejudice *n*. (prej-i-dis) a preconceived opinion; an adverse opinion that is formed before sufficient knowledge; to judge a person irrationally, based on preconceived notions, rather than knowledge of a person

prerogative *n*. (pri-rog-a-tiv) an exclusive or special right

proclaim *vb*. (pro-klaym) to declare publicly

prohibit *vb*. (pro-hi-bit) disallow

prominent *adj*. (prah-mi-nent) readily noticeable; stands out

propaganda *n*. (prop-a-gan-dah) the spreading of ideas, information, or rumor for the purpose of injuring an institution, or a person

racism *n*. (ray-sizm) a belief that one race is superior to another; belief that race is the primary determining factor in human traits

reclaim *vb*. (re-klaym) to rescue from an undesirable state; to tame or subdue

renounce *vb*. (re-nownts) to give up a birthright

rescind *vb*. (ree-sind) to take back

resist *vb*. (re-zist) to exert force in opposition; to oppose

revamp *vb*. (re-vamp) to completely make over

sabbatical *n*. (sa-ba-ti-kel) time off from teaching, often with pay

samurai *n*. (sa-ma-rye) Japanese warrior

sansei *n*. (san-say-ee) third-generation Japanese-American

scandal *n*. (skan-del) conduct that causes disgrace

segregationist *adj*. (seg-ri-gay-shin-est) to separate the races

sharecrop *vb*. (shair-krop) to farm as a tenant farmer who is provided with credit for seeds, tools, living quarters, and food, who works the land, and who receives an agreed-upon share of the value of the crop minus charges

speculate *vb*. (spek-you-layt) to guess

valedictorian *n*. (val-e-dik-tor-e-an) a student, usually having the highest ranking in the class, who delivers the speech at graduation

wage *vb*. (wayj) to engage in or carry on